See and Say
Tagalog

by Joann Javier Owens

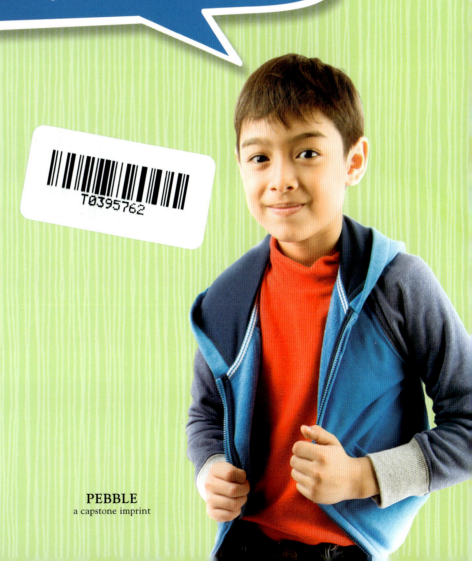

PEBBLE
a capstone imprint

Published by Pebble, an imprint of Capstone
1710 Roe Crest Drive, North Mankato, Minnesota 56003
capstonepub.com

Copyright © 2025 by Capstone. All rights reserved. No part of this publication may be reproduced in whole or in part, or stored in a retrieval system, or transmitted in any form or by any means, electronic, mechanical, photocopying, recording, or otherwise, without written permission of the publisher.

Library of Congress Cataloging-in-Publication Data is available on the Library of Congress website.
ISBN: 9780756587499 (hardcover)
ISBN: 9780756587444 (paperback)
ISBN: 9780756587451 (ebook PDF)

Summary: How do you say "Nice to meet you" in Tagalog? What's the Tagalog word for *grandmother*? With this book, curious kids will see and say simple words and phrases in Tagalog.

Editorial Credits
Editor: Ericka Smith; Designer: Sarah Bennett; Media Researcher: Svetlana Zhurkin; Production Specialist: Katy LaVigne

Image Credits
Alamy: BSIP SA, 18 (top), Kabayanmark Images, 14 (middle right); Dreamstime: Efired, 27 (top), Junpinzon, 18 (middle left), 25 (top left), Michael Edwards, 18 (middle right), Tupungato, 18 (bottom); Getty Images: DimanDiver, 15 (middle left), Gilbert Rondilla Photography, 5 (top), 14 (top), 16 (top, bottom left), 22 (middle), Images By Tang Ming Tung, 7 (top), Jun Belen, 11 (bottom), kool99, 7 (bottom right), Krit of Studio OMG, 23 (bottom left), linegold, 27 (bottom), LumerB, 25 (bottom right), OwlJustice, 15 (top), Paper Boat Creative, 6, Peter Dazeley, 22 (top), Sasiistock, 7 (middle), SDI Productions, 22 (bottom); Shutterstock: 30042000, 17 (middle left), A Stevan R L, 15 (middle right), Adam Constanza, 19 (top right), 20 (middle right), Akkaradet Bangchun, 14 (middle left), aldarinho, 21 (middle left), Amnat Phuthamrong, 20 (bottom), anatoliiSushko, 26 (middle), Anna ART, 19 (bottom left), Artyooran, 21 (bottom), asife, 31 (middle), at.rma, 25 (middle left), bergamont, 29 (middle right), bonchan, 10 (bottom), Boonchuay Promjiam, 29 (bottom left), Cardinal illustration, 14 (top right), Clara Bastian, 12 (bottom right), Dmytro Leschenko, 13 (bottom), Elena Serebryakova, 20 (top), Elizabeth_0102, 29 (middle left), Eric Isselee, 12 (top left), FamVeld, 30 (middle left), Fascinadora, 30 (middle), Fotofermer, 28 (bottom left), fotohunter, cover (top right), Fresh Stocks, 9 (bottom), halimqd (speech bubble and burst), cover and throughout, hans engbers, 25 (bottom left), hijodeponggol, 26 (bottom), Ho Thi Thanh Van, 11 (middle left), Irina Wilhauk, 31 (top), Jill Gulles, 5 (bottom), 19 (top left), 25 (middle right), junpinzon, cover (bottom left), 10 (top), 23 (bottom right), Kenishirotie, 17 (top), Kim David, 11 (top), Littlekidmoment, cover (bottom right), 1, Magnia (lined texture), cover and throughout, Markus Mainka, 21 (top), Marti Bug Catcher, cover (middle left), Martin Mecnarowski, 12 (top right), MDV Edwards, 7 (bottom left), 19 (middle left), Monkey Business Images, 8, Naypong Studio, 29 (top), Nitchakul Sangpetcharakun, 14 (bottom), nukeaf, 24, Nynke van Holten, 13 (middle right), oksana2010, 28 (top right), Pepew Fegley, 12 (bottom left), photosounds, 18 (bus station), Phuong D. Nguyen, 21 (middle right), Pixel-Shot, 5 (middle), 11 (middle right), pixelheadphoto digitalskillet, 23 (middle), Prachaya Roekdeethaweesab, 4, Q88, 9 (top), 17 (middle right), Richard Whitcombe, 26 (top), Romel Lapay, 11 (bread), Ruth Black, 30 (top, middle right, bottom), 31 (middle right, middle left, bottom), smrm1977, cover (top left), spiharu.u (spot line art), cover and throughout, SujanGurung, 23 (top), Tim UR, 28 (top left), TorwaiStudio, 16 (bottom right), Tsekhmister, 13 (top left, middle left), Tupungato, 19 (middle right), Vangert, 28 (bottom right), Walter Eric Sy, 19 (bottom right), winphong, 29 (bottom right), Wirestock Creators, 20 (middle left), Yuriy Budilnikov, 25 (top right)

Any additional websites and resources referenced in this book are not maintained, authorized, or sponsored by Capstone. All product and company names are trademarks™ or registered® trademarks of their respective holders.

Printed and bound in China. 6096

Table of Contents

The Tagalog Language............................ 4

Greetings and Phrases........................... 6

Family... 8

Food.. 10

Animals... 12

At Home.. 14

Clothing 16

In My Community 18

Transportation 20

Hobbies 22

Days of the Week 24

Seasons 25

Weather Conditions............................. 26

Colors 28

Numbers... 30

About the Translator 32

The Tagalog Language

Filipino, also known as Tagalog (tuh-GAH-log), is one of many languages spoken in the Philippines. The country actually has over 100 native languages! About a third of Filipino words come from the Spanish language because Spanish people colonized—or took control of the country—from the mid-1500s to the late 1800s.

Pronouncing *Ng* and *Nga* in Tagalog

The *ng* in the Filipino alphabet is one of the hardest sounds for people whose first language isn't Tagalog to say correctly. But it sounds the same as *ng* in the words *sing* and *wing*. To say *nga*, combine the nasal sound of *ng* with "ah." So *nga* is pronounced "ngah." The word *ng* is pronounced "nang."

How to Use This Book

Some words and phrases complete a sentence. Those will appear in bold.

English	**I like . . .**
Tagalog	Gusto kong . . .
Say It!	goos-TOH kong

+

English	**dancing.**
Tagalog	sumayaw.
Say It!	soo-mah-YOW

Others give you the name for a person, place, thing, or idea.

English	spring
Tagalog	tagsibol
Say It!	tag-see-BOHL

English	milk
Tagalog	gatas
Say It!	GAH-tahs

Meet Chatty Cat! Chatty Cat will show you how to say the words and phrases in this book.

Greetings and Phrases

Tagalog Mga Pagbati
Say It! mung-AH pag-BAH-tee

English Hello!
Tagalog Kumusta?
Say It! koo-moos-TAH

English My name is . . .
Tagalog Ang pangalan ko ay. . .
Say It! ahng pah-NGAH-lahn koh ahy

English What is your name?
Tagalog Ano ang pangalan mo?
Say It! Ah-NOH ahng pah-NGAH-lan moh

English Welcome!
Tagalog Mabuhay!
Say It! mah-BOO-hahy

English Nice to meet you.
Tagalog Ikinagagalak kong makilala ka.
Say It! ee-kee-nah-gah-GAH-lahk kong mah-kee-LAH-lah kah

English How are you?
Tagalog Kumusta ka?
Say It! koo-MOOS-tah kah

English I am fine.
Tagalog Ako ay mabuti naman.
Say It! ah-KOH ahy mah-BOO-tee nah-MAHN

In the Philippines, people use *kumusta*—which means "how are you"—as a greeting similar to *hello*.

6

English Please.
Tagalog Pakiusap.
Say It! pah-kee-OO-sahp

English Thank you!
Tagalog Salamat!
Say It! sah-LAH-maht

English You're welcome!
Tagalog Walang anuman!
Say It! wah-LAHNG ah-NOH-mahn

English Goodbye!
Tagalog Paalam!
Say It! pah-AH-lam

English See you later!
Tagalog Sa muling pagkikita!
Say It! sah moo-LING pag-kee-KEE-tah

English Yes.
Tagalog Oo.
Say It! uh-uh

English No.
Tagalog Hindi.
Say It! hin-DEE

In the Philippines, when people talk to elders or people in authority, they add "po" (puh) or "opo" (uh-puh) when answering. To say "yes" to an elder or someone with authority, you'd say "opo" (uh-PUH). To say "no," you'd say "hindi po" (hin-DEE PUH).

7

Family

Tagalog Pamilya
Say It! pah-MIL-yah

English This is . . .
Tagalog Ito . . .
Say It! ee-TOH

English my mother.
Tagalog ang aking nanay.
Say It! ahng ah-KING nah-NAHY

English my father.
Tagalog ang aking tatay.
Say It! ahng ah-KING tah-TAHY

English my sibling.
Tagalog ang aking kapatid.
Say It! ahng ah-KING kah-PAH-tid

English my sister.
Tagalog ang aking kapatid na babae.
Say It! ahng ah-KING kah-PAH-tid nah bah-BAH-eh

English my brother.
Tagalog ang aking kapatid na lalake.
Say It! ahng ah-KING kah-PAH-tid nah lah-LAH-keh

As a sign of respect, Filipino people call their older sisters (and older girls and women) *ate* (ah-TEH). For older brothers (and older boys and men) they use the word *kuya* (koo-YAH).

8

English	my aunt.
Tagalog	ang aking tita.
Say It!	ahng ah-KING tee-TAH

English	my uncle.
Tagalog	ang aking tito.
Say It!	ahng ah-KING tee-TOH

English	my cousin.
Tagalog	ang aking pinsan.
Say It!	ahng ah-KING pin-SAHN

English	my grandmother.
Tagalog	ang aking lola.
Say It!	ahng ah-KING loh-LAH

English	my grandfather.
Tagalog	ang aking lolo.
Say It!	ahng ah-KING loh-LOH

Food

Tagalog Pagkain
Say It! pag-KAH-in

English I'm hungry. I want . . .
Tagalog Ako'y gutom. Gusto ko ng . . .
Say It! ah-KOI goo-TOM goos-TOH koh nang

English breakfast.
Tagalog almusal.
Say It! al-MOO-sahl

English tapsilog (beef, garlic fried rice, and a fried egg)
Tagalog tapsilog
Say It! tap-SEE-log

English lunch.
Tagalog tanghalian.
Say It! tang-hah-LEE-ahn

English sinigang (tamarind soup)
Tagalog sinigang
Say It! see-nee-GAHNG

English dinner.
Tagalog hapunan.
Say It! hah-POO-nan

English chicken adobo
Tagalog adobong manok
Say It! ah-DOH-bong mah-NOHK

English rice
Tagalog kanin
Say It! kah-NIN

English a snack.
Tagalog meryenda.
Say It! mer-YEN-dah

English bread
Tagalog tinapay
Say It! tee-NAH-pahy

English squash
Tagalog kalabasa
Say It! kah-lah-BAH-sah

English milk
Tagalog gatas
Say It! GAH-tahs

English chocolate rice pudding
Tagalog champorado
Say It! cham-poh-RAH-doh

Rice is life in the Philippines! It's a part of every meal, including snacks.

11

Animals

Tagalog Mga Hayop
Say It! mung-AH hah-YOHP

English a bird
Tagalog ibon
Say It! ee-BON

English a dog
Tagalog aso
Say It! AH-suh

English a cow
Tagalog baka
Say It! BAH-kah

English a frog
Tagalog palaka
Say It! pah-LAH-kah

12

English a chicken
Tagalog manok
Say It! 🐱 mah-NOHK

English a fish
Tagalog isda
Say It! 🐱 ees-DAH

English a pig
Tagalog baboy
Say It! 🐱 BAH-boi

English a cat
Tagalog pusa
Say It! 🐱 POO-sah

English a horse
Tagalog kabayo
Say It! 🐱 kah-BAH-yuh

13

At Home

Tagalog Sa Bahay
Say It! sah BAH-hahy

English kitchen
Tagalog kusina
Say It! koo-SEE-nah

English living room
Tagalog sala
Say It! SAH-lah

English door
Tagalog pinto
Say It! pin-TOH

English window
Tagalog bintana
Say It! bin-TAH-nah

English chair
Tagalog silya
Say It! SEEL-yah

English table
Tagalog lamesa
Say It! lah-MEH-sah

English television
Tagalog telebisyon
Say It! teh-leh-BIS-yon

English computer
Tagalog kompyuter
Say It! kom-PYOO-ter

English	Tagalog	Say It!
bedroom	kuwarto	kwar-TOH
bed	kama	kah-MAH
pillow	unan	OO-nan
water dipper	tabo	tah-BOH
bathroom	banyo	bahn-YOH
toilet	inidoro	ee-nee-DOH-roh
bucket	balde	bahl-DEH

Buckets and water dippers are common in Filipino households. They are primarily used for taking a shower and washing up after using the toilet. Outside the bathroom, they are used for cleaning and watering plants.

Clothing

Tagalog Kasuotan
Say It! kah-soh-OO-tahn

English I am wearing . . .
Tagalog Ang sinusuot ko ay . . .
Say It! ahng see-noh-SUH-oht koh ahy . . .

English a shirt.
Tagalog kamiseta.
Say It! kah-mee-SEH-tah

English pants.
Tagalog pantalon.
Say It! pan-TAH-lon

English a hat.
Tagalog sombrero.
Say It! som-BRE-roh

English a rain jacket.
Tagalog kapote.
Say It! kah-POH-teh

16

English flip-flops.
Tagalog tsinelas.
Say It! chee-NEH-lahs

English a dress.
Tagalog bestida.
Say It! behs-TEE-dah

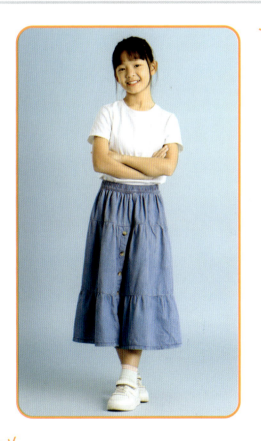

English a skirt.
Tagalog palda.
Say It! PAL-dah

English socks.
Tagalog medyas.
Say It! MED-jahs

English shoes.
Tagalog sapatos.
Say It! sah-PAH-tohs

In My Community

Tagalog Sa Aking Komunidad
Say It! sah AH-king koh-muh-nee-DAD

English a school
Tagalog paaralan
Say It! PAH-ah-rah-LAHN

English a bus station
Tagalog istasyon ng bus
Say It! ees-tah-SHON nang boos

English a grocery store
Tagalog tindahan
Say It! tin-DAH-hahn

English a hospital
Tagalog ospital
Say It! ohs-pee-TAHL

English a post office
Tagalog tanggapan ng koreo
Say It! tang-GAH-pan nang kor-YOH

English sundry store
Tagalog tindahang sari-sari
Say It! tin-DAH-hahng SAH-rih SAH-rih

English a fire station
Tagalog istasyon ng bombero
Say It! ees-tah-SHON nang boom-BEH-roh

English a street
Tagalog kalye
Say It! KAHL-yeh

English a library
Tagalog silid-aklatan
Say It! see-LEED ahk-LAH-tahn

English a house
Tagalog bahay
Say It! BAH-hahy

English a park
Tagalog parke
Say It! par-KEH

19

Transportation

Tagalog Transportasyon
Say It! trans-por-tah-SHON

English a boat
Tagalog bangka
Say It! bang-KAH

English a bicycle
Tagalog bisikleta
Say It! bee-seh-KLEH-tah

English a truck
Tagalog trak
Say It! trak

English a train
Tagalog tren
Say It! tren

20

English an airplane
Tagalog eroplano
Say It! eh-rop-LAH-noh

English a bus
Tagalog bus
Say It! boos

English a car
Tagalog kotse
Say It! koh-CHEH

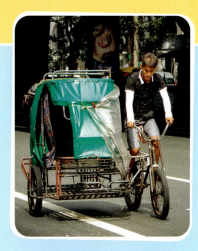

English pedicab
Tagalog padyak
Say It! pah-JAK

English a jeep
Tagalog jeep
Say It! dyeep

Jeep is short for *jeepney*. Jeepneys look like short school buses. They are the most common form of transportation in the Philippines, followed by buses and pedicabs.

21

Hobbies

Tagalog Mga Libangan
Say It! mung-AH lee-BAH-ngahn

English I like . . .
Tagalog Gusto kong . . .
Say It! goos-TOH kong

English dancing.
Tagalog sumayaw.
Say It! soo-mah-YOW

English singing.
Tagalog kumanta.
Say It! koo-man-TAH

English videoke. (karaoke)
Tagalog videoke.
Say It! vih-dee-oh-KEH

English painting.
Tagalog magpinta.
Say It! mug-pin-TAH

22

English	**basketball.**
Tagalog	basketbol.
Say It!	BAS-ket-BALL

English	a ball
Tagalog	bola
Say It!	BOH-lah

English	**reading.**
Tagalog	magbasa.
Say It!	mug-bah-SAH

English	a book
Tagalog	libro
Say It!	leeb-ROH

English	**cooking.**
Tagalog	magluto.
Say It!	mug-loo-TOH

English	**swimming**.
Tagalog	lumangoy.
Say It!	loo-mah-NGOI

23

Days of the Week

English	Today is . . .
Tagalog	Ngayon ay . . .
Say It!	ngah-YON ahy

Tagalog	Mga Araw ng Linggo
Say It!	mung-AH AH-rahw nang LING-goh

English	Monday.
Tagalog	Lunes.
Say It!	LOO-nehs

English	Tuesday.
Tagalog	Martes.
Say It!	mar-TEHS

English	Wednesday.
Tagalog	Miyerkules.
Say It!	mee-YEHR-koo-less

English	Thursday.
Tagalog	Huwebes.
Say It!	HWEH-behs

English	Friday.
Tagalog	Biyernes.
Say It!	bee-YER-nehs

English	Saturday.
Tagalog	Sabado.
Say It!	SAH-bah-doh

English	Sunday.
Tagalog	Linggo.
Say It!	LING-goh

Seasons

Tagalog Mga Panahon
Say It! mung-AH pah-nah-HON

English wet season
Tagalog tag-ulan
Say It! tag-oo-LAN

English dry season
Tagalog tagtuyot
Say It! tag-too-YOHT

English winter
Tagalog taglamig
Say It! tag-lah-MIG

English spring
Tagalog tagsibol
Say It! tag-see-BOHL

English summer
Tagalog taginit
Say It! tag-ee-NIT

English fall
Tagalog taglagas
Say It! tag-lah-GAS

Weather Conditions

| Tagalog | Lagay ng Panahon |
| Say It! | lah-GAHY nang pah-nah-HON |

English	It is . . .
Tagalog	Ito ay . . .
Say It!	ee-TOH ahy

English	windy.
Tagalog	mahangin.
Say It!	mah-HAH-ngin

English	raining.
Tagalog	umuulan.
Say It!	oo-moo-oo-LAHN

English	cold.
Tagalog	malamig.
Say It!	mah-lah-MIG

26

English hot.
Tagalog mainit.
Say It! mah-EE-nit

English sunny.
Tagalog maaraw.
Say It! mah-AH-rahw

English cloudy.
Tagalog maulap.
Say It! mah-OO-lahp

Colors

Tagalog Mga Kulay
Say It! 🐱 mung-AH koo-LAHY

English red
Tagalog pula
Say It! 🐱 poo-LAH

English pink
Tagalog kulay rosas
Say It! 🐱 koo-LAHY ROH-sahs

English green
Tagalog berde
Say It! 🐱 BEHR-deh

English orange
Tagalog kahel
Say It! 🐱 kah-HEL

English blue
Tagalog bughaw
Say It! boog-HOW

English yellow
Tagalog dilaw
Say It! dee-LAHW

English black
Tagalog itim
Say It! ee-TIM

English white
Tagalog puti
Say It! poo-TIH

English purple
Tagalog kulay ube
Say It! koo-LAHY oo-BEH

29

Numbers

Tagalog Mga Bilang
Say It! 🐱 mung-AH BEE-lahng

1
English one
Tagalog isa
Say It! 🐱 ee-SAH

2
English two
Tagalog dalawa
Say It! 🐱 dah-lah-WAH

3
English three
Tagalog tatlo
Say It! 🐱 tat-LOH

4
English four
Tagalog apat
Say It! 🐱 AH-pat

5
English five
Tagalog lima
Say It! 🐱 lee-MAH

6
English six
Tagalog anim
Say It! 🐱 AH-nim

7
English seven
Tagalog pito
Say It! 🐱 pee-TOH

8
English eight
Tagalog walo
Say It! 🐱 wah-LOH

9
English nine
Tagalog siyam
Say It! 🐱 sham

10
English ten
Tagalog sampu
Say It! 🐱 sam-PUH

About the Translator

Joann Javier Owens is a multilingual children's book author. Having kids inspired her to publish books that talk about her homeland and its culture. When she's not writing, she enjoys spending time with her boys outdoors.